Contents

Introduction

In this world there are many people, including business people, who want to make a difference for the good of all, for the good of the planet and for their own good. Heart based Creativity is a way to do just that.

There are ways of using the Mind in order to be creative. But using the Heart has several advantages over the Mind in this process, an aspect of which can be summed up by a phrase I once heard, "the Mind suspects, the Heart knows". It is through the heart you can have access to a higher quality energy and information than is available through the mind. This is explained in more detail in the introductory sections which explore the advantages and consequences of Heart based Creativity.

There are also guided meditations that can be used for Heart based Creativity, and meditations that have the purpose of supporting and strengthening you in this creative process.

May you be successfully creative.

Heart based Creativity

Ever wanted to do something creative, and there was feeling of frustration, there was a block? No matter how hard you pushed and made an effort, nothing creative came of it? This can be a really annoying feeling.

Creativity cannot be pushed, though it can be coaxed.

Some years ago, I came across a range of techniques that were loosely termed accelerated learning. There was a great deal of information on how the brain worked, and on how learning and creativity could happen. There was some really useful stuff, though not much of it seeped through into the mainstream other than fragments. Ways of supporting creativity included brainstorming, and connecting up branches of ideas on paper, which was sometimes called drawing spider-diagrams. The techniques were useful ways of using the mind and catalysing creativity. One fun, yet powerful and even relaxing way to come up with some new and novel ideas, was to use a creative visualisation. This would involve the students relaxing with eyes closed and following the visualisation in their own imagination. In the visualisation they would go someplace or a series of events would happen to effortlessly generate a new idea or understanding. The students could then use what they experienced in their creativity and work. It was great fun and productive at the same time.

Over the years I've come to realise though, that it was all very much "head" stuff, it all focused on the mind. It was all to do with mindpower, which at the time was quite fashionable, and to some extent, still is. I wondered if there was another step; a better way.

I also found myself thinking a lot about what creativity is. In basic terms, I began to think of there being a creative impulse, which could come from a variety of sources. This would be picked up by the person, who would then do something with it, and give it an expression.

Creativity became anything that a person expressed in order to bring something new into the world. This could be a piece of art, or music or literature. It could also be the plans for a building, a new business, a new product, a new tool, a new therapeutic technique, or a social event.

A piece of creativity has a context, a background it fitted into. The creator may (or may not!) have some idea of the value of their creation, and an understanding of how it can fit in with the world. This bit got me pondering. Through what I had learnt, I knew that the mind only understood the world and life through the lens of the past, because that was all it had to go on. I knew that its understanding was limited to experience, and blinkered to the breadth of that experience. Then understanding was filtered through one's prejudices and favourite ways of thinking. The beliefs a person held depended in great part on when they were born and where. So a person born in a South American rainforest a thousand years ago would hold very different beliefs and ways of thinking to a person born twenty years ago in London; this implies there is a local fashion in thinking, depending on where you live, when you are alive, languages available, and your culture.

The mind simply was not up to the job of sensing the big picture, it only held in its own way a fragment of the past. What would have access to the big picture? Well, the heart.

The heart centre or chakra, is a place where the soul resides. The soul is part of a very large group of souls called the Oversoul, which is part of God, Who happens to know the Big Picture.

So instead of focusing on the mind, with its limited picture, what you do is focus on the heart centre, with its link to the Big Picture.

By focusing and "being in your heart", and then using a meditation or creative visualisation based on the heart, you can connect with a creative impulse that is just right for you, and which fits in the Big Picture.

Heart based creativity helps you be creative in a way that ends up being good for you, for those around you and the community, and for the planet, as it is based on love.

The creative impulse might show you something simple and straightforward, or uniquely different and original. Whichever way, it will be just right.

Being Spiritual and How to be Creative with the New Energies

A big part of practical spirituality is being creative. One way we can be creative is to access the huge store of new creative energy within us. We can touch this through guided meditation. We can feel into it and explore it in our inner world, and then express in many ways in the world out there. Put another way, we first go into our inner world, sometimes beyond what we know, receive a spark of creativity, let this transform through our body, and then move it out into our outer world. Sounds simple, and it is.

Spirituality enables us to connect with beauty and love, and blend this with a creative mix of order and chaos to create something new in our world. This creativity can have spiritual depth, integrity, and spiritual usefulness.

The link between spirituality and creativity is important right now. Times change and spirituality changes. The highlight of spirituality used to be sitting in silence, meditating for hours at a time in a cave, in an ashram, in a monastery, or at home. That's the old way. Now it's about living our everyday life with a foundation of spirituality. It's now about living the spiritual energy, which can be done anywhere, and it's about how we live with a sense of rightness and love. Meditation may or may not be a part of this, though for some people it is very important. It can be useful and an excellent help in living fully in the outer world. Meditation has long had a role in being immensely helpful with creativity, and now is more so.

In today's world, living spiritually can now mean being creative. As spirituality is about how we live, this means being creative in a way that is filled with love, harmony and beauty, so that the creativity expresses these qualities.

People can be creative in countless ways. Planting a wood, recording a song, writing, setting up a business, writing computer software, making jewellery, doing science in a new and loving way, doing art... the list of ways of being creative is endless.

Often, what passes for creativity is a rehash of the old. So we get old-style formulaic music, repetitive fashions, old ideas in areas of human life re-expressed, art that is devoid of new insights and possibilities, and science that lacks love. Sameness is familiar, comfortable and easily accepted, and empty. Change is the unknown and scary, and is filled with opportunity and new horizons.

We can all be creative, and we all approach creativity in unique ways. People have a head (mind) and a heart. How we approach creativity energetically will affect our creative efforts, and it's like a sliding scale. We can be all head, through to 50% head and 50% heart, through to all heart. A lot of the ways of accessing new ideas and creativity, such as can be found in the worlds of business, education and therapy, rely heavily if not exclusively on the head, on the mind. Mind has its limitations. As mentioned earlier, if you were born in a different time and different place, with different experiences to learn from, you would think differently to how you do now, perhaps you would speak another language. Your mind would perceive the world differently to how it does now. When you thought, you would come up with ideas that would suit your mind uniquely for that place and time, but not for right now. The mind has generally been past-orientated and limited, dependent on the experiences available. The mind's perception is limited, and the creative output from the mind is limited.

The heart centre, however, is a different story entirely, and it is a spiritual story that touches on what it means to be human.

In your heart centre resides the energy of your soul. Souls incarnate in Creation on the plane of consciousness they have evolved to, over a series of reincarnations. That means that in "young souls" with not that many lifetimes under their belt, the level of consciousness of the souls isn't actually that high. Old souls will have reincarnated several millions of times in human form, so the consciousness of their soul will be high (but way below that of God-realised souls). Now this is in Creation, which is in Time. Outside time, it's a different matter, and a tricky one to totally grasp. Outside time, on the inner planes, the soul can touch other souls more experienced, and from that vantage point, advice can then be offered on its progress reflecting the lives already lived in Creation. Meanwhile in Creation, the soul is limited by its experience. Fortunately, we are going to get some help here from that aspect of soul that is outside time on the inner planes, that has access to what you need.

The soul is also part of the Oversoul, which is like a huge collective of an incredibly large number of souls, which are essentially "fragments" of God, though God can never be fragmented. These souls are like bits of God with some sense of individuality. The Oversoul is part of God.

Whereas the mind learns from what is around it in the world, and bases its thinking on this (and thinks it knows everything), the heart is a doorway to the soul, to the Oversoul and to God. The heart then is an amazing place, it is a doorway to brand new, ever-changing energy and information and creative impulses, that are completely in step with what is happening right now. The information found in the heart comes from a source that has an overview, the big picture, of what is going on in the Universe and on the Earth, in the past, right now, and in the future. The information is also individualised and specific to each person and their lives. The creative energy available within this is very high quality.

Creative energy means change. Change can happen in many ways. Often in life, it can simply be what happens to us. The impact can be minimal through to completely life-changing. In many cases people have no choice about the change and just have go along with it. The path it leads onto may or may not be a fulfilling path.

Letting creative energy flow in a deliberate way happens by choice, and this can create change in ways that are fulfilling, and increase our levels of happiness. This is helped by deliberately letting go as much of the old as seems right, to create the space to move forward; it creates a lightness of energy around us.

Being creative can be an adventure. Being creative by accessing the creative impulses through your heart means being on a creative adventure that is completely aligned with what is the highest option for yourself. It means being on a high-quality timeline, which is part of what is called the Golden Pathway timeline.

If accessing the creative impulse in your heart becomes a way of life, it means you become open to the rapid changes in energy which you can bring into your life.

Connecting with the creative impulses and information in your heart is actually quite easy, and quite natural when you practice it. Plus it's something you learn more about by doing and by experience. In this way you learn to understand the process and learn about the inner world in your heart. This applies to everyone. Everyone has a heart centre, everyone has a soul that is part of the Oversoul and God, and we can all learn to access this birthright.

To assist with this process of creativity, it helps to focus on the heart as a first step. So instead of meditating on the head centres, we simply place our awareness on our heart centre in the middle of the chest, and keep paying it attention. This seems to feed and energise the heart centre, and lets it become more energised. Twenty minutes a day of this heart centred meditating is a very good preparation for creative meditation.

The basis of connecting with the creative information and impulse is to go into this upper part of the heart centre, like putting your awareness into a wonderful space, and then accepting the packages of energy, opening them up, and letting this energy flow into your being. Being relaxed and allowing and trusting the process is a big help. Thoughts, feelings, images and sounds about the creativity may be apparent straight away, or it may take its time to filter into your awareness, so allowing the process to flow is important. It isn't something that can be forced.

With practise and as you become more sensitized, it becomes easier to pick up the information being offered.

That's the inspiration part. Next comes the focus and effort to bring this creativity to fruition. If it is a big project, you can use the heart-centred creativity meditations on smaller aspects of the project as you go along.

The Need for a Heart based Vision

A significant part of being creative is having a vision of what you want to do, and how you want an aspect or all aspects of your life or business to be like. The vision provides direction and shows you the steps to take. Usually linked with your vision is the emotional desire, the drive and the emotion, the will if you like, to see this through.

Vision takes into account what you already know. This includes what you know about the opportunities available for your business, your niche, the state of the competition, known and projected developments in the business you are in, political factors, local and international economic factors, and environmental factors. These are all very obvious and usual pieces of knowledge you may have. Vision can also include a sense of something that would seem utterly without basis, such as a big risk you may need to take, yet it has a sense of rightness about it. You could call this a gut knowing at a basic level, or an intuition.

A great deal of knowledge is based on experience so far. Hence it is backward looking and based on the past. Knowledge is past orientated, even when it is projected into the future. Looking into the past is not a powerful generator of vision, of creativity or of advancement. How many developments in business or any other sphere of human endeavour have been based on the past? How many times have businesses and other organisations felt the impact of factors that were not predicted by past-orientated knowledge, even when it has been projected forward in time?

Knowledge is to do with the Mind. The amount of knowledge available to the Mind is limited. What knowledge there is perceived through a belief system or a set of beliefs, for example, economic theories, which in part make up "conventional wisdom". Conventional wisdom is limited and in no way refers to the future, or the complexities of the present.

The Mind cannot take into account all possible viewpoints, as it lacks the awareness and ability to understand in depth. Hence the vision that comes from the Mind is limited. It relates to the Big Picture only a little, and mostly not at all.

When you have an intuition or a gut feeling, that is tapping into a tiny part of the Big Picture, and you find you take the steps that prove to be right.

The way to access relevant information that does relate to the Big Picture in a deep way, is to access it through the Heart, by this is meant the heart centre or chakra, in the middle of the chest.

The Heart is like a doorway through which you have access to those aspects of the Big Picture that pertain to you and your organisation on a need-to-know basis, with a very personalised and individual nature. You get the information, and the vision, that you personally need to have.

The Heart, and everything that comes through it, has to do with Love, and with Unity. The information and vision you can pick up from the Heart, comes from a source that knows all things to be unique, all things to be connected, and for all things to be Love. The Heart is also to do with courage, Hope and Trust. There is no fear tainting the viewpoint.

This is quite different to the conventional viewpoint that has as a basis of business activity the idea of competition, of doing what it takes to not be overtaken, to look good, to achieve at whatever cost, the fear of not surviving, in some cases, to see customers as cash-cows and as people to be exploited, and perhaps to see the workforce as numbers and as people to be used, rather than see them as human beings.

If you access information and vision through the Heart, it will be based on Love, and on doing what is right from a loving point of view. This will apply for all concerned; yourself, the workforce, the customers, any shareholders, the local community, the local environment and the planet. It has to do with service and giving, and as it is in a business context, on receiving in return some form of energy, usually in the form of money at the moment. It is at its very root a loving based attitude rather than a fear based one. All of this comes inbuilt into the information and vision from the Heart, and that is a powerful thing. The Mind suspects, the Heart knows, as I once heard.

This loving perspective applies to long-term vision, and any smaller aspects of the vision such as you might connect with at the start of the day before the day's activities. When you act from information and vision that comes from the Heart, your actions will be moving in the right and loving direction, to have an impact in an increasingly positive way. When you act in a way that is right, for what feels like the right motivation, then your energy expands, and your aura brightens.

A heart based vision can be analysed in depth as well, to give more understanding. This leads to wisdom in actions undertaken. The whole process of continually upgrading your heart based vision is an on-going learning process.

The more you use a heart based guided meditation, such as described later on, to access a vision for your Business (or life), the more you get a feel for how to do it. Once you have started this process and have a big chunk of vision, you could if you wish deliberately ask to be shown information and a vision which sheds some light on the impact of your activities on the environment, or how best to work with your workforce, or your shareholders, or your customers, and so on. You may ask for information and a vision relating to the raw materials you use, or the financial markets (the financial weather). You will get a feel as to what area to look into, and how the meditation needs to flow.

Your heart based vision will flow and change, and keep moving on, like life. So regularly updating and questing into it is useful. What you will know is that you are operating from a vision based on Love, and the Big Picture.

Rewriting the Scripts - Doing Business in New Ways with New Values

This could be a time for completely reinventing how business happens, how people think, feel and behave in a business, and why they do that. Accessing information through the heart can be a very powerful catalyst for this process.

There are a number of strands to doing business in new ways with new values. One is doing what is right, another is about how you interact with and treat people, and the third is about how your business does things. These three strands are inter-mixed and have a bearing on each other.

Business is about people within the business, and people and organisations outside the business. Running your business in a creative way based on the information you gather through your heart can mean changing how you relate to people, and changing what you do with them. If you use heart based creativity meditations in considering people within and without the business, you may find that you get more of a sense of what people need from you and the business.

For those people inside your business and should it be necessary, if you change the way you treat people, and change what you do for them and give them, you might find they work differently and their creativity changes; they will treat you differently.

You may or may not make changes, though if you use your heart as the source of creative impetus, it can be a case of "follow your heart" and have faith in what you gain from your meditations, and let this guide your actions. With regards to having faith, in life we have faith in some things that we use to guide our decisions. These can be newspaper reports and opinions, what we read and see on the Internet, what we hear from other people, and what we see for ourselves. We always put our faith in something, even if it is a default action. So in making decisions or acting in a certain way, you can deliberately choose to put your faith in your own heart and the information you gather from using your heart. Using heart based creativity requires the trust and the faith to use it as a process of letting go, and letting in something new. This should tally with a sense of rightness as well, but this doesn't mean that any decision that comes out of it won't occasionally seem a risk or a long shot. Where there is an intuitive rightness, it may not be immediately apparent what the value or the importance of the action is, and this will unfold over time.

The same applies for those people outside of the business, yet who have a relationship with the business. These people will also have needs as to how they need to be treated and interacted with.

The people whose needs we might want to consider in our relationships with them will include customers, suppliers, potential customers and potential suppliers, and people connected to these. It will include local communities or groups of people further afield.

Accessing heart based information will influence our knowing of what to do for them and alongside with them.

Accessing information through your heart may have an effect on your business. Perhaps it means running the business differently and restructuring it in new ways. This would require a flexible approach from everyone, a willingness to embrace change, and ways of getting everybody aboard. Perception is important, and actions might make no sense to those outside observers who have not taken part in the meditation, so for those people who need to know, a way to rationally explain what you are doing may be necessary.

In this world, in everyday life, people think and act according to personality, experience, past events, and personal values and beliefs. What people think and do is mostly driven by the subconscious mind plus some other very interesting factors. For ourselves, accessing information via the heart is something different, and can take us outside of what makes us up as a person.

In thinking about other people, the fact that everyone is different means that they all need something different. We may wonder about the wisdom of treating a person a certain way depending on what we have discovered through a meditation for heart based creativity, but we really don't know the bigger picture for them, so we need to trust. We do this knowing that the guided meditation approach goes beyond the personality and all the other factors, it transcends them to come up with something more far reaching, and very suitable for them.

Treating people in a new way, for reasons gained through the heart, will bring about changes over time as to how you do business, and about what it means to do business.

If you use heart based creativity in business then the focus shifts as to why you do what you do. Rather than doing what is usual or traditional or the conventional wisdom in business, and what is safe or comfortable, it means doing what you do because it is right. You go with what comes out from the information you have found through the meditation, and trust the processes and bring in creative solutions.

This ties in with the people aspect of your business. In meditation you might find there is a future high chance of a business relationship not being suitable or successful. Then you might find there is a case for curtailing or certainly keeping a close eye on a business relationship. Additionally, you might find there is a case starting up or deepening a relationship.

From a 3-D, everyday point of view, at times there might not be an apparent reason, but in the long-term and according to the big picture which you access, your decision and actions will make sense. There should also always be a sense of rightness though, with what you are doing, and if not, check using heart base creative meditation again.

Hopefully it is becoming evident that there is a powerful intrinsic value in using heart based creativity in business. We usually make decisions and take actions based on what we know. There are limits to what we know. In fact, we don't know much, and right now we are living in a world that is changing in very surprising ways, politically, technologically, weatherwise, financially, geologically, and in subsequent, follow-on ways, such as in global food production. The past is not a guide to the present or the future as everything changes. Good quality information that is suitable for yourself comes from that doorway of the heart, so you can access the opportunities and the new approaches to business and to life.

The third part of doing business in new ways with new values involves looking at what you are doing now and how you do these things. What needs to change? What on the surface looks fine but needs to change?

What you are doing here is noticing what needs to come in, what is becoming obsolete or even dangerous and needs changing. It's essentially about noticing what is desirable to change so that what you do is appropriate, reliable and successful.

Using heart based creativity to gain information on all aspects of your business and its workings means that you can know what to change given that there are changes in the world around you that affect your business, and that will affect your business in the future. The information you access automatically takes into account the bigger picture. It means also that you notice where improvements can be made for an improved future.

An example of changing to take into account external influences is a business that uses electricity, where at the moment the costs are high, but into the near future the costs will become higher, affecting outgoings, and so profits. By noticing the issue, the business can already start to respond to the situation. For example, energy costs become a factor in profitability. There is a growing case for minimizing energy use, and if possible, even generating energy and breaking the link with the energy companies, so that profitability is maintained.

Another issue could be that of giving and receiving payment, locally and internationally. Looking at this issue might come up with more stable ways of acting when buying or receiving payment. For example, using heart based creativity, it may be apparent that in a situation that barter is the best option as a system of payment, and in some cases, doing something for free for the sake of helping with a project or helping a business is a good option.

Then there are the issues of providing a service or services, or making and selling a product. If you provide a service, you may want to consider the service you provide. Is it up-to-date? Do you provide it in the best way possible or is a new way required? Is there scope for a new product? How is the market?

Is it changing and are there new possibilities for who you can sell to? Is there different technology you can use to support you in providing the service you do? Are there ways of improving the service or services?

With creating a product, you can gain useful information as to how your product sits in the big scheme of things. Is it viable? Can it be improved? Is there something new to make and sell? What is the best way to make your product? What is the best way to get it to your customers?

With a product, you could analyse that product in as much detail as you want, including looking at the processes you use to create it, at the materials you need for them, the individual components of them, the way you store them, and so on, Similarly, you can dissect what goes into a service and how it is provided to the customer in as much detail as you need.

As you use the heart based meditation techniques you learn to get a feel for what to focus on and expand into. Generally, you learn to go with the flow of the meditation, rather than try to force it, and in this way, you can tend to get the information that is useful.

The Guided Meditations

There are 5 types of guided meditations on the following pages:

1) To help you build your connection to your heart centre.

2) To improve and boost your heart centre

3) To generating positive change in your chakras and energy system

4) General guided meditations to access information from the heart centre on your own or in a group

5) Heart based creativity meditations for aspects of a new or existing business

A more in-depth explanation is given before each set of meditations, though you will gain a greater understanding by doing them!

Meditations to help you build your connection with your heart centre

The first set of meditations are all about connecting with the heart centres and becoming more and more sensitive to them. These are fantastic meditations to do for everyday life as well as for experiencing the heart centre more in meditation. Being in your heart helps you to experience life in a loving and love-filled way. Your heart centre is also an amazing source of creativity. One of the greatest gifts you can give yourself is a deep connection with your heart centre.
These meditations are great to do more or less everyday.

Meditations to help you build your connection with your heart centre

Connecting with your heart centre meditation 1

This is one of the main meditations. The more you use it, the better. You connect more and more with the heart, and become increasingly
sensitive to what's in there. You become more sensitive to the most loving choices, decisions and activities to do. The more you have a connection with your heart centre the more you know what is right for you.

Ideally, this meditation should be done everyday. For best results, do it in the morning and the evening. It strengthens focus and increases ability to be aware of the heart centre, and work with it.

In a comfortable position and with your eyes closed, put your aware- ness in the centre of your chest, just inside the ribs and behind the sternum bone. You might sense the heart centre as a feeling, or even as a sphere of energy that is peaceful and calm. It might have a colour. For five minutes, simply put your awareness on this space; this energy. Notice how it feels. You might be aware of a sense of energy flowing, of a restfulness and a gentleness. It may feel very peaceful.

Keep resting your awareness on this centre. If your attention drifts come back to the heart centre with your focus. Place your focus on this centre again, and continue for the five minutes.

When you have finished, imagine there are two doors in front of this heart centre. On the front of each door is a beautiful white rose. Close the doors, so the white roses show from the front. Now become aware of the rest of your body and open your eyes.

After practising for five minutes each day for several days, you may like to increase the meditation time to 20 minutes.

Meditations to help you build your connection with your heart centre

Connecting with your heart centre meditation 2

Focusing on the heart centre opens it up and brings through it more energy and more love. When you can feel into situations with love, and have that love influence thinking, then more right thinking happens. The heart centre or chakra is connected to quite a power source, though not power in the way it is thought about and used down here. It's more the power that drives everything in Creation.

Find a comfortable place, where you can relax and focus without being disturbed. Take several deep and gentle breaths to enable you to take your awareness away from the outer world, and the sensations in your body, so that you can focus your attention on your heart centre in the middle of your chest.
Imagine there is a bright and powerful source of light at the very centre of your heart chakra, rather like a star, or a super nova. It shines very bright and very powerfully. Simply keep your attention on this star or super nova, and allow it to shine out the energies from within it. Allow these energies to wash through your heart centre, and then on out to other parts of your body. Let yourself keep focused on this for three minutes or so.
When the three minutes are complete, bring your awareness back out from your heart centre, and into your body, and observe your breathing for several breaths. Then open your eyes.

You can do this meditation everyday, or alternate it with the first heart meditation. It is a very powerful introduction to using guided meditation for heart based creativity, and is also far more than that.

Improving and boosting the heart centre

The second section has in it meditations to improve and boost the heart centre. The heart centre is a chakra, and like all chakras, it can be healed, upgraded and basically have its functioning ability improved. Working with these meditations does just that. This means improved creativity. These meditations can be used everyday at first, and then every so often.

Improving and boosting your heart centre

Guided meditation to boost the energy in your heart centre

Your heart centre can receive upgrades of energy.
This meditation is a fantastic way of bringing in the very best energy for your heart centre.
In a comfortable position close your eyes and put your attention on your heart centre in the middle of your chest.
Imagine a white rose coming down, from a position very high up and directly above you. This white rose holds a powerful and beautiful special energy.
Imagine this white rose comes down through the top of your head, through your neck and chest, to come to rest in the middle of your heart centre. This white rose radiates out love and light in through your heart centre. This heals and transforms your heart centre. Allow this white rose to be there as long as necessary. You may feel wave after wave, or pulse after pulse of healing light.
This allows healing love to flow into your body. You may want to do this for several minutes.
When you are ready, become aware of your body, and open your eyes.
You can do this meditation quickly or for up to five minutes. It is a very powerful meditation and very healing.

Improving and boosting your heart centre

Guided meditation to clear the heart centre

Heart centres are just like other chakras in that they can become clogged up with energy you don't need. In order to have your heart centre working properly it needs to be clear, which can mean cleaning it up. The guided meditation below is a straight-forward way of cleaning your heart centre. The time it takes to clean up becomes less with practice.

In a comfortable position with your eyes closed, focus on your heart centre. Imagine it has nine layers to it like an onion has layers.

Notice if there are colours in the outer layers. Ideally each layer should be colourless. White light flows down directly from above you, through the top of your head, through your neck and chest, into the outer layer of the heart centre. The white light fills the outer layer (call it layer 9) and washes it through. After a few moments the white light flows into the next layer, layer 8, washing that through. After this layer has been cleared, the white light flows into layer 7. When this is clear the white light flows into layer 6, washing and cleaning, and then into layers 5, 4, 3, 2 and the central layer 1.

The white light from up above fades and you sense and feel the difference in your heart centre. Become aware of your body now, and when you are ready, open your eyes.

Improving and boosting your heart centre

Bringing down Blue Light into the Heart

This is a way of bringing in powerful, up-to-date healing energy into your heart centre and into your system generally. It really boosts your heart centre. The blue light is a new type of energy and is very healing in a way that improves and upgrades your energy system. There is also some focus on the head, the brain, and the other centres in the head as they too are involved in the process of creativity. This is a meditation that can be repeated periodically to bring about more improvement, as and when it feels right.

In meditation, place your focus on your heart centre. Imagine that from directly above you and from high up, comes down three drops of liquid blue light. The three drops land on your head. One drop stays in your head while the other two travel down into your chest. One drop goes above your heart centre and the other drop goes into your heart centre. The blue light from all three drops expands out. The blue light in the head expands to fill the brain, the glands (pineal and pituitary) in the head, and the chakras in the head. The blue light heals and updates the brain, glands and centres. The blue light heals the space above the heart centre, and expands and heals your heart centre. Let yourself experience the effects of the blue light for several moments.

You may find a residue of blue light remains in these areas now. When you feel the process has ended, become aware of your feet, and the rest of your body, then open your eyes.

Improving and boosting your heart centre

A colourful flower in the heart

Chakras can be given updates of energy, and this guided meditation is a way of gaining such an update.

In meditation, imagine forming in front of you a flower with five petals of different colours. The centre of the flower is a shining bright white colour. The colours of the petals from the top are yellow/gold, white, blue, red and green. The colours may mix and swirl, creating a dynamic pattern of all colours. The flower of colours goes into your heart centre. The flower then radiates out light of a variety of colours appropriate to your needs, for as long as is required. You might find the yellow/gold light flows in first, or the red flows in; it depends on your unique needs for right now. Let the flower do what it needs. When the process seems complete, sense the heart centre and sense any changes. Become aware of your body, and open your eyes.

Generating positive change in your chakras and energy system

Your energy system is made up of your chakras (with particu-lar emphasis on the heart centre), the layers of your aura, and your nervous system, which plays a vital part in handling incoming energy including on an everyday basis.

As you improve or upgrade your energy system, you are able to process the information and energy you pick up in an en-hanced way. This translates into being able to pick out more detail, being able to handle more energy, being able to process what you pick up in a more refined way, and be able to under-stand the information in increased depth. Doing these guided meditations basically leads to improved ability to pick up and process the creative information and energy, and make the most of it. There are added benefits in day-to-day living from having an upgraded system as well.

The following meditations will help improve your energy sys-tem overall and improve creativity.

Generating positive change in your chakras and energy system

A Crucial Meditation: Heart Wrapping Around the Head

This is a crucial meditation. The heart has access to a greater amount of information than the mind. This means that choices made with the heart's input are made from a greater knowing than just relying on the mind, which is limited in its ability to make choices and decisions on its own. This meditation is about wrapping up the mind so that the mind works as a tool of the heart, so that it works properly.

Imagine a blue flame filling the space around the heart centre. Watch this blue flame for a while, and feel the emotions in it. Now blue light spreads out from this flame to form the bottom part of a shell of blue light. The blue light of the shell spreads outwards then upwards to grow up and over your head. The blue light that started in the heart area then flows from the shell of blue light into the head, into your brain, the outer cortex, the mid-brain, and the lower brain stem. The blue light flows all the way through your brain until it turns blue. Allow the blue light to flow here for a moment. Then when you are ready, open your eyes.

Generating positive change in your chakras and energy system

Guided meditation to tweak the system (Quite an important one)

Once you pick up creative energy and information, it goes into your system and is processed. Your system can be thought of as your chakras, your aura, your brain, your nervous system, your thoughts, feelings and beliefs; in fact everything that makes you up as a person. This next meditation is aimed at making some changes in how creative energy and information is processed.

Go into meditation and focus on your heart centre. Let it glow gold and let the energy swirl around it. Now small lines of gold light shine out of the surface of your heart centre, which radiates out a calming and uplifting energy. Next, sparks of gold/white energy that are like tiny spirals shoot out at several points over the heart centre, and flow into your body, bringing in new qualities. Your heart centre then glows brightly and intensely white, and a pulse of white light flows through every part of you. Your heart centre then settles down and glows a gentle gold colour.

Bring your awareness now to your body. When you are ready, open your eyes.

Generating positive change in your chakras and energy system

Gold Light

This is a straightforward yet powerful meditation that is useful in preparing yourself for the heart based creativity guided meditations.

With your eyes closed, focus on making your breathing even. Now imagine that you look inside yourself and you see a mist. Flowing down from high above you comes a bright gold light. It flows around you to form a layer of gold light. More bright gold flows down and flows in through the top of your head, through your body and into the mist. Particles in the mist start to sparkle, while others disappear in a puff of smoke. The gold light keeps pouring into and around the mist, which starts to alter its shape, becoming straighter, and the sparkling particles start to take up a shape that is brighter and more graceful. You might be able to sense how that feels, and the effect it has on your overall energy. Notice the effects for a while, you might be able to put words to them.

Allow the gold light that is around you and in you to remain. Now look for energy packages around you that look like black butterflies. The gold light becomes tinged with white and blue, and as it flows around you and in you, it blows off the black butterflies away from your space and dissolves them. Flowing down with the gold light with tinges of blue and white are brilliant white butterflies which are positive energy packages. These go to the areas where they are needed. Let them flow to these places, settle and pass on their energy to you. When you are ready, open your eyes.

Generating positive change in your chakras and energy system

Guided meditation to balance the four elements, earth, air, fire and water

It helps if you balance the four energetic elements, earth, air, fire and water, both in your space and in your being, as we all have a key beneficial affiliation with one of these elements. This is a preparatory meditation which has a positive effect on our energy.

Close your eyes, and place your awareness in the middle of your chest, in your heart centre.

Firstly, a blue light flows down and fills your heart space. After a while it settles down to form a stage or platform. On this stage comes forward the energy of each element. The energy of the element earth appears. You might notice the feel it has. Then the energy of the element air comes onto the stage. Again notice how it feels, and how it makes you feel. The element of fire arrives. Again, try to get a sense of how that feels and how it makes you feel. Finally the energy of the element water appears. How does this feel, and what effect does it have on your energy?

Multi-coloured light flows down into your heart space onto the elements and fills them. Three elements then step back, and one of them steps forward. As more multi-coloured light pours down, the energy from the element at the front expands and spreads out into all parts of your body for several moments. Become aware of how this feels, breathe it into all parts of you for as long as feels necessary. When you feel complete, let the energy of the element recede. Make a mental note if you can of the element that interacted the most with you.

When the process feels complete, open your eyes.

Generating positive change in your chakras and energy system

Gold stars meditation

Close your eyes and relax. Focus on the centre of your chest, where your heart centre resides. Imagine this heart centre as a ball of light. Let yourself simply notice this for a few moments. Now let your awareness flow into your heart centre, into this ball of light. Once in your heart centre, a space opens up around you. Allow yourself to be in the space and feel the qualities in your heart centre.

Then from very high up above in this heart space, comes down a flow of small gold stars. They come into the heart space and float there. Simply observe them.

Several of these gold stars then flow up and out of your heart centre, and into your head, your throat and your upper chest, where they make their home. They shine out a steady, constant flow of gold around them.

Several of the gold stars floating in the heart centre then float down into the lower part of your body and legs. Again they settle and glow with a constant gold light.

Two of the gold stars move from the space in your heart centre down your legs and onto the soles of the feet.

You find yourself with what looks like a golden pathway below you. The gold stars on the soles of your feet attract you to the pathway and pull you onto it, and help you maintain your connection to the golden pathway. Feel the effects of this for a few moments. Energy and qualities flow up from this pathway into and through your feet. Feel the qualities and energy flowing in, along with the opportunities and the quality of adventure that comes with being on this path.

Bring your awareness back to your heart centre and rest here for a while. Then bring your awareness back into all of your body. Feel your fingers and toes. When you are ready, open your eyes.

Generating positive change in your chakras and energy system

Clearing Thoughts, Emotions and Energy When Times are Testing

Occasionally life can be tough, and rather than being happy, relaxed and clear, we can be upset, confused, and with thoughts and emotions flying through us. It's hard being creative when we are like this, so we need a way through. There are a variety of ways, and this is a guided visualisation way, best done after doing something like physical exertion to shift the energy from your physical body. This guided meditation is based on the energy in the Earth. Some people enjoy going to hot springs where there happens to be hot, black mud. They sit in it, and cover their faces in it. This mud and heat helps them relax, unwind, and calm down. Even detox. Some people enjoy going for a walk in Nature and relax that way. Basically put, the Earth's energy is very good for us. In this meditation, we won't be using black mud, but restful, slow frequency black light from the Earth to clear out the more frantic and chaotic energies in our systems.

Go into meditation and imagine yourself sitting on the Earth. Imagine growing thick roots out of the base of your spine, and out of the soles of your feet, deep into the ground. Make the roots a dark colour that is grounding, such as dark blue, dark green or dark brown or black. Imagine the roots growing as deep as you can. See the discordant energy in your body as black and perhaps even as slimy energy. Now allow thick black light from the Earth to flow up your roots. This energy is slow, restful, and nourishing to your body, as you have a strong connection with the Earth since the atoms in your body come from the Earth. The Earth's black light gently and slowly makes its way up your legs into your body, then it flows into your arms and head. As it does this, a point of brilliant and pure white light forms at the top of your head. The black light from the Earth starts to fall back down towards the Earth, and as this happens, it takes with it the discordant black energy from your system. The point of white light glows and sends down pulses of white light that help push the black light through your feet and base of your spine, back into the Earth.

More black light from the Earth rises up again through your roots, feet, legs, and body into your head. As the Earth's black light flows up through your organs you might feel the restful effect it has on them. You might feel the restful effects it has on your bones and muscles, and on your mind. It can feel like sitting in a warm mud pool. The energy is nourishing, and cleanses out negativity to help restore balance in your system. The point of white light sends out more pulses like ripples of white light, to help the slow frequency black light flow back into the Earth.

Once more the black light flows up your roots, in through your feet, to slowly rise up your body, and dissolve away and remove the discordant energy. When the black light reaches the top of your head, the point of white light once again sends out pulses of white light, to help move the black energy out through your feet.

When this is complete, become aware of your body, your arms and legs, and fingers and toes, and when you are ready, open your eyes.

This meditation is also good to do before going to sleep, and is excellent to do while in Nature, particularly after spending too much time at the computer.

For a variation, you could soak up the Earth's black nourishing light into your body, and let it stay there all night, or all day for a restful time.

Accessing the Creative Information from the Heart

The third section of meditations contains techniques for accessing the creative information and impulses that can flow through the heart, with its access to the infinite and to original concepts that you can then express in new ways.

You may find you have a favourite meditation or you can vary the method you use to bring in the creative energy and information. Over time you might find the meditations naturally evolve and change of their own accord. This is fine as it keeps the meditations up-to-date and fresh. These meditations can be used at the start of a project and at points throughout it. They can also be used when a particular situation arises in life or related to learning, creativity and work.

With all the meditations you could read them through first and then try them out, or record yourself reading a meditation so that you can play it back, or have another person read them out to you. To get the most out of them, do them in a comfortable, quiet place where you won't be disturbed. Do them with eyes closed, though whenever there is a need, open your eyes. Try to sit still, and have as much silence and stillness inside you as possible. Enjoy the guided meditations, and enjoy your creativity.

Accessing the Creative Information from the Heart

Meditation to Access a Creative Pulse

Imagine you can sense your heart centre in the middle of your chest. Imagine it grows larger. Gently a doorway appears in it. The doorway is rimmed with brilliant, sparkling white light. You step through this doorway into a glowing space of white light. Notice this for a moment. In front of you, you see a Golden Pathway. Step onto this and take a few steps.

Look around you and you will sense, or see, feel, hear, smell, packages of energy and of creative information. These may appear as wrapped presents, balls of light, treasure chests, books, sparkles of light, etc. Choose one of these packages of energy and of creative information and go up to it. Imagine placing your hands on it. Energy then pulses and flows from the package into your heart centre. Notice this. It then flows out into the rest of your body. As it does this, become aware of images, sounds and emotions associated with the packages of energy and creative information. The energy then flows up into your head. It then works its way around circuits in the brain and nervous system. Again, you may become aware of the information and of any feelings and thoughts linked with it.

Creative energy flows in its own time, so let yourself be patiently aware of the energy, and allow the visual information, or the sounds, or feelings, tastes or smells, or movements to come to you.

Now imagine walking back out of the heart through the doorway rimmed with white light. Stay aware of the thoughts and feelings which are aspects of the energy you have accessed that are held in your system.

As and when you need to, come out of meditation. You may want to write down any ideas that have come through.

Accessing the Creative Information from the Heart

A meditation to access a heart based vision

Sometimes in life it's right to have a Purpose to your life, and a Vision of how you want an aspect of your life to be, to go with this Purpose. The vision may be a picture of how things could be. Or it could be a series of snap-shots over time, or like a video of how events progress along a timeline. Usually a vision will be visual, though there may be sound and emotion and other sensations. The vision comes from the purpose. There is purpose which can be someone else's idea of what you should be doing, or there can be a vision coming from a purpose based on personality needs and wants. Sometimes a Purpose and Vision literally lands on a person, and appears in great detail.

There can also be a Purpose that comes out of the heart, and a Vision that comes out of the heart to go with it.

Heart based creativity meditations will show creativity related to your Purpose. It will either allude to it, or show you clearly what your unique Purpose is. In some respects you don't need to spend time digging in to the information that you get to find your Purpose. You can work with the creative information that you are given instead, which will be fine. If your Purpose becomes apparent, that is also fine. Besides, what we understand as our Purpose won't be as detailed or as comprehensive as the Purpose as it is understood by the heart or by the Soul, or at a higher level.

So here is a meditation to connect with a heart based vision.

In a quiet place, close your eyes. Feel your feet and toes, and imagine them sending out roots deep into the ground. Deeper and deeper they go, until they connect with the peace and tranquillity of the Earth. Feel that for a few moments, and feel it travelling up and into your feet. Feel this travel up into your body, and your head. You might find that a stillness flows up with the peace and tranquillity into your body.

Now, from high above you, flows white light, down in through the top of your head. Wave after wave flows in, travelling further inside you each time. The waves of white light flow into the middle of your chest, and into your heart centre, washing it with wave after wave of white light.

After a while, your heart centre opens up, and you can see inside it is filled with glowing white light. Let your awareness flow into your heart centre and image you are inside your heart. The white light washes through you; brilliant and clearing.

From within the middle of your heart centre flows towards you an image of what to do creatively. Out flows a word, as a sound or as an image. This word may be on its own or it might expand into several words that are to do with your vision. Let yourself relax and allow the information to flow as it needs to flow, and trust this flow. The word or words can act as a doorway later, and can be expanded upon even more.

Out of the centre of the heart now flows an image, or a symbol, which again can act as a doorway. This time, let your awareness flow into it and then into another space. Feel what it feels like here in this new space, what the emotions feel like, because the emotions are like fuel which energise your vision. Notice any thoughts or ideas that are here, to give you more of the picture. Notice the feel of the intention inside this vision energy. Now, let any other information in the form of sounds or images flow to you.

Let the word or words to do with the creativity flow to you again. This time imagine flowing your awareness into them, like going through a doorway into another new space. Allow yourself to just *be* in that energy, absorbing it. Notice how your heart feels with this energy and information linked with the creativity. Then let any more images or sensations flow to you, and into you.

Next, imagine a pathway forming in front of you all about "being" on this pathway, and about "doing" any actions that present themselves. This pathway is a timeline, a timeline of your purpose. You may see or feel ahead of you some of the actions to take, or events that can happen. Allow whatever information that needs to appear to appear. Bask in this for a moment.

Now let yourself flow out of this space and back into your heart centre. Take a look around your heart space, and feel any emotions or intentions in here that the meditation has produced.

Next let your awareness flow back into your body. Feel the waves of white light washing down through you. Then feel the peace, tranquility and stillness flow into your body through your feet to help you stay grounded and centred. Feel this for a few moments.

Then, when you are ready, open your eyes.

You can come back to this meditation anytime.

It's best to do it in a very quiet place, and have silence inside yourself. Silence is inside you because God is inside you, and your heart is a doorway for the soul, and the soul is a part of the Oversoul, which is part of God. You can always tell when God visits because there is an incredible and beautiful silence, all around and inside.

Accessing the Creative Information from the Heart

Offer a Situation Up, Receive a Creative Answer

This works great if you have a situation where you need more under- standing, and a solution. Before doing this meditation, think of the situation to which you want a creative answer. Think of it in such a way that you could at least partially describe it to some other person. If you are confused about a situation and don't know how to grasp it, in your thoughts say something like, "I'm confused about ...", and offer this up in the meditation.

In a comfortable place, close your eyes, and breathe gently and deeply for several breaths. In meditation, imagine wrapping the situation in white light like a bubble. Then offering it up, and let it float upwards, and upwards, to a pair of white-gloved hands. The hands take the situation up into the light.

Now focus on your heart centre glowing white. This centre expands and in the middle of this a hole like a doorway ap- pears. In this doorway a white-gloved hand appears holding a ball of bright, glowing white energy. This white light from the ball shines out into the heart centre, offering emotional under- standing and insights. The glowing white light then flows up into the head bringing insights into what can be done.

When you are ready, come out of meditation, and make notes if you need.

This meditation is great for when you want a creative input to improve a situation that you feel could be better, or to start off a project that is brand new.

Accessing the Creative Information from the Heart

Being Creative in Challenging Times

It is easy to be creative when you are living in a "reliable" world, when we are comfortable and not challenged. The big trick is to be creative in unfamiliar environments and when everything seems to change and take us beyond our comfort zone. The mind is sometimes not very good at coping in times like this, but the heart with its love, trust and connection to the big picture, can cope. As long as we can keep our emotions calm. The more we practise being creative in unfamiliar environments, the easier it gets.

This meditation is about going deep enough into the heart to cope and be creative.

Close your eyes, get comfortable, take several deep and gentle breaths. In meditation, focus on your feet, let roots grow out of your feet deep into the Earth to anchor you. Let your roots grow as deep as possible so that you root into the ground thoroughly. Let pulses of calming Earth-energy flow up your roots to play their part in soothing your nervous system and body.

Now focus on your heart centre in the middle of your chest. Imagine it pulsing out colours. These colours swirl into your body and head, again calming you. Now let your awareness go inside your heart centre, into a calm, silent and still, white space. Let your awareness rest there for a while. Then allow any image or images, feelings, words or other sensations flowing into you, to show you a step or action to take. Trust what you are given in this space. The trust is important so that your heart wins out over any suggestions from your head. When you have received enough information and perhaps any symbols to think about, bring your awareness out of the silent and still white space. Focus into your body, and when you are ready, open your eyes. You may want to note down what you experienced.

Accessing the creative information from the heart

Shooting Stars of Creativity

Shooting stars are lumps of rock, extra-terrestrial rock, that come flying into the Earth's atmosphere at very high speeds from outer space, after a very long journey. These meteorites bring something new into the planet Earth.

Think of a topic you want to be creative about, or alternatively, allow yourself to let in whatever creativity is there for you.
Close your eyes. Imagine placing your awareness in the middle of your chest. Imagine it as a space which is silent and still. At first a star shines blue/white light down through the top of your head, down through your body, into this space, filling it with starlight. Imagine going into this space in your heart and the space expands and becomes huge. You look up and see the stars. As you gaze up at the stars, a rock travels at very high speed across the sky. You see it as a streak of white light moving very fast. The light from this seems to flash towards you and quickly imprint through your eyes and into your heart. It's as if you get a message very quickly in a very short burst. Hold the energy and the information inside you, and allow it to unfold bit by bit into your awareness, relaxing as you allow this to happen.
When this feels complete, bring your awareness out of your heart, and into your body, and your fingers and toes. Open your eyes, and make notes if you want to.

Accessing the Creative Information from the Heart

Connecting with a tree!

Meditation can be approached creatively, as long as there is a reason behind it. Gardens are fertile places full of life, full of the vitality and creativity of Nature. They can be places of beauty and inspiration, and can be a place where people work along-side nature to create something very splendid. In this meditation, there is a garden in the heart, and in this garden there is a fruit tree, with fruit on it.

Close your eyes. Allow golden sunshine to shine down through the top of your head, and through your body, into a space in the middle of your chest, into your heart centre. The sunlight shines upon a garden. This garden is beautiful, and looks wonderful in the sunshine on this summer's day. Look around the garden. Breathe in the aliveness and the fertile creativity of your garden. Walk further into your garden, and imagine standing on the soil or grass or vegetation. Feel the garden beneath your feet, feel the sunshine on your body.
You see in front of you an ancient and wise tree with fruit on it. Go to the tree, touch the trunk. Imagine you can feel the life in this tree, and imagine you can feel through the trunk the roots going deep into the Earth. Imagine, as you touch the trunk, that you can feel the sunshine landing on the leaves, passing into the tree the energy and light from the sun, and passing in inspiration and creativity.

Now go to a branch that is hanging down. Choose a fruit, and pick it. The fruit is like a package of energy and creative information. Thank the tree, and eat the fruit; take your time. As you eat, relax and let the creative emotions and the thoughts, the pictures and the sounds, and anything else about the creativity come to you.

Allow the time for the creativity to unfold itself in you.

Now, come out of the garden, and out of your heart, and bring your awareness back into your body.

When you are ready, open your eyes. Make notes if you want to.

Accessing the Creative Information from the Heart

Creativity in a Group

Groups can be creative, so long as the right people are in the group.

There is a right path, a right place and right action for everyone. With group creativity working with the heart, it works best if everyone who should be there, is there, and no-one should be there if it's not really the right thing for them, and consequently for others. Put another way, everyone is on a timeline. We all have many possible timelines. Each time line has its own energy, and its own series of moments to be gone through and experienced. A useful thing is to be on the timeline that makes us the happiest, which can mean taking action to achieve this. Sometimes peoples' timelines come together so they share a moment in time and space. If someone is off their best timeline and on the wrong timeline, then they end up either not being involved in the moment when they should be, or they are wrongly involved, which distorts it for others. The best way to be on the right timeline is to be in your heart, rather than your head, then you'll know what's right for you.

Group creativity means everyone coming along without preconceived ideas, and without agendas of their own. Everyone needs to be, or at least needs to be willing to be, in their heart. Everyone can have a heart connection and make a contribution. The creative energy and information coming through makes no distinction about a person's popularity, or how forceful they are as a personality (which in fact can be a draw- back as will may dominate heart). What counts in someone's contribution is the quality of heart in it.

A good way to start a session of group creativity is firstly for everyone
to have socialized and shared a bit, and if necessary, dealt with any emotions that need to be let go rather than have them be carried over into the creativity session.

Then there could be a meditation to help everyone really be in their hearts.

The issue or topic or project that is to be the focus of the creativity can be talked about, and more or less defined. When there is consensus or agreement about the focus of creativity, a meditation can be done to bring in the creative energy and information. If needed, everyone could take notes, and then what has been found could be talked about and any planning done.

Accessing the Creative Information from the Heart

A group meditation for group creativity

Often in group creativity, there can be several contributions made by members of the group that add up to a whole picture. This meditation is about the members of a group picking up various points of the creative information and bringing it together. This can be quite a fun activity.

As a group, firstly use one of the meditations about focusing on the heart centre. Then talk about the topic or issue you wish to be creative about.

Then in meditation, focus on the heart centre. Imagine bright white light coming in through the top of the head and flowing down into the heart centre, which then glows. Imagine a doorway forming in the heart centre, then flow your awareness through this doorway, into a glowing white space. In there, find an object, which can contain or have on it some information. Explore the object in detail. Imagine opening, or reading or listening to, or feeling the information.

Take your time. Imagine being able to touch the energy of the information and have it flow into you, which may trigger feelings and thoughts. Now bring your awareness out of your heart centre. Feel your body, then your fingers and toes and when you are ready, open your eyes. You may want to jot down some notes.

The next step is to share in turn with the other group members what your object was like, and what information with respect to creativity was in or on your object. You will probably want to talk some more about what everyone found, and piece it together into a creative solution or activity.

Heart Based Creativity Meditations for Aspects of a New or Existing Business

These meditations focus on discovering creative information from within the heart on issues relating to business. They can provide a big sweep of information, such as the intention and values behind a business which can colour all of its activities, to specific details, such as ways of selling, or ways of approaching the accounting process. The solutions and information you come up with will be completely congruent with the values in your heart, and the energy, intelligence and spirit that flows through your heart like a doorway. In this way, you and your activities become part of, and aligned with, the loving big picture.

Heart Based Creativity Meditations for Aspects of a New or Existing Business

Meditation for information about people in your organisation

If there are many people in your organisation, one way of organising everyone is to group them by what they do, so you treat them as groups in the meditation. Key people and those with critical functions can be treated individually. Another approach is to go into meditation and see who appears at that time. This would work well for small organisations. You may want to write down what you find out in the meditation. Remember that the information you find will be from your heart, so the intent is loving.

With your eyes closed, focus on your breathing for several breaths, allowing your breathing to become gentle and deep.
Then focus on the space in the centre of your chest; just noticing it for several moments. Now put your attention on your feet, and imagine very dark blue energy, like thick and bendy cables, flowing down through the floor and then through the ground and into the earth. This is for grounding and stability.
Now return your awareness into the centre of your chest, and visualise the space starting to grow brighter and lighter. Imagine it opening up like a doorway, and allow your awareness to go inside, rather like putting yourself inside your own heart space, or putting a camera inside you so you can see what is happening.
Now see a person, or a representative of a group of people, come towards you. They give you a covered box, like a gift of

information about them. The box floats in front of view. If there is any wrapping and any decoration look at this non-judgementally. Notice the quality of the wrapping and of the decoration. What does it look like, feel like, sound like, smell like and even taste like? What do you think it says about the person, and about how they relate to you. What does the shape of the box show you? What are the qualities of it?

The box opens, fast and enthusiastically, or slowly and reluctantly, or a quality in between. How does it open, what is the quality of how it opens?

Now the inside of the box presents itself to you. Without judgement, observe. What is it like? What is inside the box? What do you notice? Use all your senses to examine the box and its contents. What qualities are there, and what does this tell you about the person or group of people, and how they relate to you?

Now from behind you comes a box, like a gift, from you to that person or group of people, that they need from you, that is right for them to have in the context of the big picture. Again without judgement, use all your senses to observe any wrapping, and get a sense of the qualities. Now let the box open up, and again observe what's inside by looking, hearing, feeling, smelling and tasting. What is it you could give them? Is there a timing that feels right? What is the sense of rightness like? Are there any other impressions?

Re-wrap the gift and give it to them. Notice what seems to happen to them.

Now let their image and energy fade.

Allow another person or group of people come forward. Again, notice the box they give you and examine it as before. Then observe the box you could give them, and what happens when you do give it to them.

Do the meditation with another person or group. Stop when you have finished or when you start to tire.

Open your eyes and make your notes.

If there is any doubt about what you sensed, leave the meditation for a day or so, and then focus on the people or group of people you want clarity on, in as relaxed a way as possible. This is a powerful meditation and you grow in skill the more you use it. It is a good idea to try this meditation out with people you are familiar with at first, to gain experience.

Heart Based Creativity Meditations for Aspects of a New or Existing Business

Meditation to gather information about people and groups of people external to the organisation

The heart based meditation is very similar for the one concerning the people in the organisation. Again, remember that the information you find will be from your heart, so the intent is loving.

Before you start you may want to list key individuals and key groups of people that you know about. This is the known. You may like to make a list about people and groups that don't yet have a known connection to your business, as they might in the future. These lists can be local, regional, national and international.

The information you find will be a snap-shot of how interactions can be for the very best right now, given how life is for everyone concerned right now. The picture changes with time as people may or may not go along their optimal path because of the choices they make and the decisions they make. It's an ever evolving situation, so play what is in front of you, and "check in" using this meditation every so often, so you have up-to-date information. Basic rule: everything changes.

You can use the same meditation as before, or try this next one (which you can also use with people within the organisation).

Organisations as well as people send energy to each other. The amount of the energy flowing varies, as does the qualities of the energy. The qualities signify what is being sent, and received, and needs deciphering. You could think of a person, and think what you are doing for them, and think of the intention that is behind that. Imagine being connected by a flow of energy to that person, and imagine what you give them as a flow of energy, coloured or flavoured by your intention behind what you give them. Imagine the flow of energy from them, and look through it or feel through it carefully. Some people analyse energy by treating it as music, and listening to the quality of sound to get an idea of the qualities. What is being used here is information that is processed differently to deliberately thinking about it.

What we do in this meditation, is to access the heart, and then use the high level, loving intention of the heart which has access to the big picture, to give out the best energy, and analyse what that means.

Get comfortable, close your eyes, and take several deep and gentle breaths, feeling the energy in the breath flow all around your body, including to your fingers and toes.

Now place your attention on the centre of your chest, where your heart centre is. Visualise this appearing like an increasingly bright ball of flowing light. Now imagine a flow of gold light coming down through the top of your head, and another flow of gold light coming up from below your feet, and both flows meeting in your heart centre. Imagine a space like a doorway opening up in this ball of light, so you can flow your awareness inside. Let yourself bask in the qualities of your heart, and the qualities that can flow through into your heart from your soul, and from higher up in energy than that.

With your awareness inside your own heart, think of an organisation or a person, and imagine them being inside this space too. Inside your heart, a flow of energy forms from you to them. Notice the qualities of it and the intensity of it. Notice how you feel having this energy flowing from you. Sense as you can, what this flow means in practical terms in the everyday 3-dimensional world. What is it that you can do for them, or give them, or say to them. Trust your impressions. You may also notice the impact this flow of energy has on them. There may be changes in their emotions, and in how close they move or how far they move. Each relationship you have with this person or organisation is different and unique, and is dynamic.

You might notice that as well as being about building and improving relationships, it can also be about ending them.

You can also notice the energy flow from the person or organisation you are focusing on. Most likely, there will be some change as the energy you can give out impacts on them. If you like, analyse the qualities and what this implies in the 3-dimensional everyday world.

When you feel you have gathered enough information about what it is you need to give or do, and the intentions behind this, you can let the person or organisation either fade or go off into the distance, and allow another person or organisation appear. Once more, allow a flow of energy touched by your heart to form between you and the other person or organisation. Go through a similar process as before.

Repeat this for as long as you want to.

When you are complete for the moment, let the space in your heart become clear, and just filled with heart energy. Then bring your awareness back out of your heart space, and allow the doorway to cover over with light. Bring your awareness back to your body, and focus on your fingers and toes, and your breathing for several breaths. Then open your eyes.

Heart Based Creativity Meditations for Aspects of a New or Existing Business

Meditation to assess directions and actions, accessing the bigger picture

Before doing this meditation, think of an area of your business that you want to focus on, and the amount of detail you want to go into. This sets the scene. Alternatively, if you want to get a sense of how you are doing in several departments, in the meditation, once your awareness is in your heart, you can imagine there are several doorways to open and look in. a healthy department will look like a well ordered, happy even beautiful room. This will mean little or no change is required.

Close your eyes and breathe gently and deeply for several moments. Then place your awareness on your heart centre in the middle of your chest. Imagine your heart centre as a flame, and keep watching the flame for a few moments. Allow a flow of gold light to come down from very high up, through the top of your head and into your heart, into the flame. Simultaneously, there is another flow of gold light flowing up through your feet from the ground and into the flame that represents your heart centre.

Now imagine the flame opening up into a doorway. Let yourself flow your awareness into your heart centre. Imagine firstly that a white/gold light sprays out from the centre of your heart, covering everything in the space in energy like white/gold dust, including yourself. Now look around, and if it is appropriate that you gain an overview of several departments, see several doorways. Otherwise, if there is only one issue, there should be only one doorway. Open one doorway. Take a look in to see how the space looks, and feel the atmosphere of the room or space. If it looks pleasing to you, and has a happy, positive atmosphere, then that department or issue is fine. If it is not, then there are some changes to be made.

The room looks onto the centre of the heart. From the centre travels out a ball of light, energy and information. It comes into the space or room, and flows around to make changes for the better which are optimal changes. Put your hand on something that has changed, and allow feelings, images, sounds and perhaps words to flow up your arm. Get a feel for what the changes mean. Let yourself allow the information to flow through you.

Another ball of light, energy and information might flow into the space or room, and again make changes. Once more, put your hand out to the change and let the feelings, images and any sound and words flow up to you.

More balls of light might flow out from the centre of your heart. Each time this happens, sense with your hand the changes and the information within the changes.

When this issue or this department has received all the energy it needs, come out of that space. If this was the only issue, or if you are tired, then come out of the meditation at this point following the usual procedure. Otherwise, go to the next doorway and open it.

Once again, go into the space or room and look around, and get a feel for the atmosphere. Once again, from the centre of your heart flows a ball of light to land in this space, this room, and generate change, bringing at the same time useful information. Again, hold out your hand towards what has changed, and allow the energy, feelings and information to flow up your arm. Allow words, images and feelings and any sounds to flow to you. Again more balls of light might flow into the space, and again use your hand to pick up information on what has changed.

Repeat this procedure for any more doorways which relate to departments or issues within your organisation.

When you are complete, or need a rest, bring your awareness out from your heart centre, and focus on your breathing for several breaths. Become aware of your body, then open your eyes. Make notes if you want to.

You may find the ideas that come out of these exercises as being surprising, though you may also already have had an inkling of what needs to be done, which just means you are tuned in to your heart and more.

Once you have an idea of what to do, write it down, think about it, and flesh it out if need be. There should be a sense of rightness, and a sense of happiness in your heart about it.

The next point to consider is timing; when to take action, when to achieve your goal or target by. One way of doing this is to draw a timeline, and place the action you need to take on a place on the timeline that feels right, and there should be a feeling of being happy and excited. Your heart will know.

Also, it's sensible to start off with heart based creative meditations on something small, something not important or critical, unless you really have to. Apply commonsense and down-to-earth thinking. This means you can still be highly creative and unique, though it will come from a centred and grounded place, and stands a greater chance of success.

About the author

Jonathan Barber likes to help people make changes in their lives for the better, helping them find the best path for themselves, and then stay on that path. As part of this he aids them in getting in touch with hitherto unsuspected attributes inside themselves, and in expressing latent abilities. His aim is to assist people in expressing who they really are, which makes life richer.

He lives in South Wales with his family, and enjoys meditation, yoga, beaches, woods and hills.

For more meditations, articles and news, take a look at www.lovelightandjoy.co.uk.

Made in the USA
Charleston, SC
10 February 2012